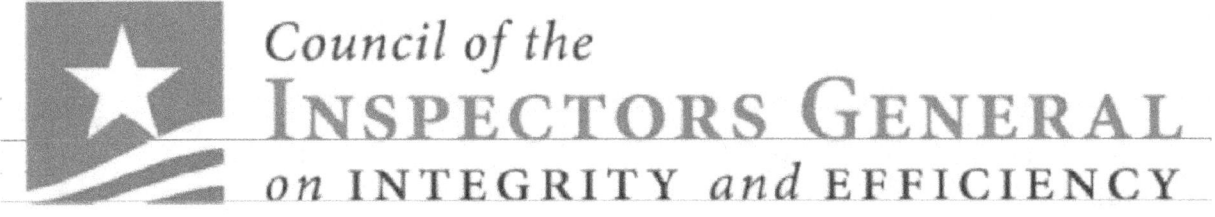

Council of the
INSPECTORS GENERAL
on INTEGRITY *and* EFFICIENCY

QUALITY STANDARDS FOR INVESTIGATIONS

November 15, 2011

Council of the Inspectors General
on Integrity and Efficiency

Authority: Section 11 of the Inspector General Act of 1978 (5 U.S.C. app. 3.), as amended.

Mission: The mission of the Council of the Inspectors General on Integrity and Efficiency (CIGIE) shall be to address integrity, economy, and effectiveness issues that transcend individual Government agencies and increase the professionalism and effectiveness of personnel by developing policies, standards, and approaches to aid in the establishment of a well-trained and highly skilled workforce in the Offices of Inspectors General.

CIGIE Investigations Committee: The Committee contributes to improvements in program integrity, efficiency, and cost effectiveness Governmentwide by providing analysis of investigative issues common to Federal agencies. The Committee provides the CIGIE community with guidance, support, and assistance in conducting high-quality investigations. Provides input to the CIGIE Professional Development Committee and the Training Institute on the training and the development needs of the CIGIE investigations community. The Committee actively engages the Assistant Inspector General for Investigations Committee to assist in carrying out the Committee's goals and strategies.

Message From the Chairman of the
CIGIE Investigations Committee

The Quality Standards for Investigations (QSI), since their inception in 1997, have successfully guided the Inspector General investigative community in producing high-quality investigations. They were modified in 2003. This 2011 version will continue to guide the community in high-quality investigative work.

The Inspector General Reform Act of 2008 (IG Reform Act) provided that members of the Council of the Inspectors General on Integrity and Efficiency (CIGIE) "shall adhere to professional standards developed by the Council" (§ 11(c)(2) of the IG Reform Act). For this 2011 edition of the QSI, the Investigations Committee has made technical changes that bring the document into full compliance with the IG Reform Act, including replacing all references to the "PCIE" (President's Council on Integrity and Efficiency) and the "ECIE" (Executive Council on Integrity and Efficiency) with "CIGIE."

The crafters of this QSI version, as did their predecessors, recognized the unique mission and varying statutory responsibilities of each CIGIE member. As a result, each OIG will adhere to the QSI in accordance with its unique mission, circumstances, and department or agency.

Throughout this version, you will also note a few minor changes for clarification, such as the definition of "periodic training." Appendix C was also added as a handy, non-exhaustive list of laws and regulations relevant to investigative work.

I want to thank the Assistant IG for Investigations (AIGI) Working Group for their diligence in soliciting input from the AIGI community and in preparing the QSI. I also want to thank the Investigations Committee for their watchful eye in finalizing the QSI. The members of the AIGI Working Group and of the Investigations Committee are listed in Appendix D.

Carl W. Hoecker
Chairman, Investigations Committee
CIGIE

TABLE OF CONTENTS

Page

PREFACE...1

GENERAL STANDARDS..2

    A. Qualifications..2
    B. Independence..6
    C. Due Professional Care..8

QUALITATIVE STANDARDS...10

    A. Planning..10
    B. Executing Investigations..11
    C. Reporting..13
    D. Managing Investigative Information.................................14

APPENDICES

    Job Task Illustration for Investigators...............................A
    Training Profile Illustration for Investigators ....B
    Non-Exhaustive Table of Legislation, Executive Orders C
    AIGI Working Group and Investigations Committee Members........D

PREFACE

The standards and principles in this document, commonly referred to as Quality Standards for Investigations (QSI), provide a framework for conducting high-quality investigations for Offices of Inspector General (OIGs) affiliated with the Council of the Inspectors General on Integrity and Efficiency (CIGIE).

Recognizing that members of the OIG community are widely diverse in their missions, authorities, staffing levels, funding, and day-to-day operations, certain foundational standards apply to any investigative organization. As such, the standards outlined here are comprehensive, relevant, and sufficiently broad to accommodate a full range of OIG criminal, civil, and administrative investigations across the CIGIE membership.

OIGs will incorporate the standards and principles outlined here into an operations manual or handbook. This should be accomplished in accordance with the OIG's particular mission, unique circumstances, and respective department or agency requirements. OIGs are encouraged to monitor changes in the laws, regulations, and other guidance cited here and revise their policies as necessary, pending future releases of the QSI. In the event the QSI are found to be inconsistent with laws, rules, regulations, or other pertinent official pronouncements, the latter take precedence.

The QSI categorize investigative standards as General and Qualitative. General Standards address qualifications, independence, and due professional care. Qualitative Standards focus on investigative planning, execution, reporting, and information management.

This QSI supersede the standards published by the President's Council on Integrity and Efficiency and the Executive Council on Integrity and Efficiency dated December 2003.

QUALITY STANDARDS FOR INVESTIGATIONS

GENERAL STANDARDS

General Standards apply to investigators and the organizational environment in which they perform. The three general standards address qualifications, independence, and due professional care.

A. QUALIFICATIONS

The first general standard for investigative organizations is:

> *Individuals assigned to conduct the investigative activities must collectively possess professional proficiency for the tasks required.*

This standard places upon the investigative organization the responsibility for ensuring that investigations are conducted by personnel who collectively have the knowledge and skills required to perform the investigative activities.

Guidelines

Investigations vary in purpose and scope and may involve alleged violations of criminal or civil laws, as well as administrative requirements. The focus of an investigation can include the integrity of programs, operations, and personnel in agencies at Federal, State, and local levels of government; procurement and grant fraud schemes; environment, safety, and health violations; benefits fraud; the background and suitability of individuals for employment or a security clearance designation; whistleblower retaliation; and other matters involving alleged violations of law, rules, regulations and policies. Some of these investigations address both civil and criminal acts, ranging in significance from a misdemeanor to a felony. Others involve administrative misconduct issues. They often require using specialized investigative techniques; examining complex financial transactions, contracts, grants, and business operations; and interviewing government and corporate officials. A wide variety of skills and extensive knowledge are necessary to perform the broad range of activities required by these diverse investigations.

Investigative organizations should establish criteria to be used in recruiting and selecting the best qualified applicants. At a minimum, factors to be considered in employing entry-level candidates should include: education and experience, character, physical capabilities, and age. Each of these factors may be controlled by legislation, regulation, or agency needs. Investigative organizations should review these criteria to ensure that they assist in providing the best qualified applicants. In addition, organizations should establish appropriate avenues for investigators to acquire and maintain the necessary knowledge, skills, and abilities; complete entry-level training, participate in in-service training; and receive professional development opportunities.

Education—It is desirable that all newly appointed investigators possess a 4-year degree from an accredited college. The knowledge acquired from a higher education will enable the investigator to deal with complex problems encountered in day-to-day investigative work. Higher education enhances the investigator's ability to communicate effectively, both orally and in writing, with witnesses, other law enforcement agencies, prosecutors, supervisors, coworkers, and the public.

Experience—Depending on the specific needs of the agency, allowances may be made for candidates to substitute job experience for a college education. Suitable job experience would provide the candidate with demonstrable knowledge, skills, and abilities pertinent to the investigative position as discussed later in this document. Depending upon the nature of the investigative organization's mission, additional requirements may be established for specific types of experience (financial skills, computer skills, etc.).

Character—Each investigator must possess and maintain the highest standards of conduct and ethics, including unimpeachable honesty and integrity. Every citizen is entitled to have confidence in the integrity of Government employees, particularly investigators who routinely access sensitive information and execute search and arrest warrants. Further, investigative personnel may be subject to statutory and legal requirements relating to integrity (Giglio, Lautenberg, Brady,[1] etc.). Consequently, OIGs should establish sound hiring policies to adequately screen applicants for investigative positions. Processes to consider include, but are not limited to, criminal history checks, queries of commercially available databases, drug testing, personal interviews, previous employment and reference checks, and background investigations.[2]

OIGs should also have policies that require investigative personnel to report any arrest, conviction, or other potential misconduct issue that would jeopardize their performance of duties. Such policies may also include requiring investigative personnel to be subject to periodic criminal history and background checks.

Physical Capabilities—Each investigative organization should develop job-related physical or medical requirements consistent with current statutes, regulations, and

---

[1] See *Giglio* v. *United States*, 405 U.S. 150 (1972); Lautenberg Amendment, 18 USC Section 922(g)(9); and *Brady* v. *Maryland* (1963) 373 U.S. 83.

[2] The Office of Personnel Management (OPM) categorizes background investigations as National Agency Checks with Inquiries (NACI); Moderate Risk Background Investigation (MBI); Background Investigation (BI), and Single Scope Background Investigation (SSBI). Please refer to OPM for further guidance.

agency policies to enable investigators to discharge their duties, while promoting personal well-being.

The physical demands placed upon the investigator will vary among agencies. OIGs employing criminal investigators should establish a physical fitness program to provide and maintain physical fitness and reduce the risks of cardiovascular disease, obesity, stress, and related ailments and disorders.

It is in the interest of an investigative agency to establish and maintain a vibrant workforce because an investigator's duties frequently require irregular unscheduled hours, personal risk, exposure to extreme weather, considerable travel, and arduous exertion. Investigators are frequently engaged in stressful encounters and can be victims of stress-related medical disorders.

Age—Consideration should be given to minimum and maximum age requirements for entry-level criminal investigator positions in accordance with applicable statutes and regulations. Waivers may be granted only in accordance with applicable regulations.

Knowledge, Skills, and Abilities—Because of the critical and sensitive nature of an investigator's position, investigative agencies should ensure that all investigators, commensurate with grade level, possess the requisite knowledge, skills, and abilities summarized below to fulfill their responsibilities.

1. A knowledge of theories, principles, practices, and techniques of investigation and the education, ability, and experience to apply such knowledge to the type of investigation being conducted;
2. A knowledge of government organizations; programs; activities; functions; and, where applicable, their interrelations with the private sector;
3. A knowledge of applicable laws, rules, and regulations, including the U.S. Constitution; the U.S. Criminal Code (including elements of crimes); the Federal Rules of Evidence; the Federal Rules of Criminal Procedure; and other pertinent statutes, such as the Privacy, Freedom of Information, and Whistleblower Protection Acts;
4. An ability to exercise tact, initiative, ingenuity, resourcefulness, and judgment in collecting and analyzing facts, evidence, and other pertinent data; apply sound deductive reasoning; and deliver oral and written reports;
5. An ability to safely and effectively carry out law enforcement powers, where duly authorized, including carrying firearms, applying for and executing search warrants, serving subpoenas, and making arrests; and
6. The skills necessary for the investigation. This qualification standard recognizes that proper training is required to meet the need for the broad range of special knowledge and skills necessary to conduct investigations. This training should include both formal classroom and on-the-job training. The qualifications listed below apply to the skills of an investigative organization as

a whole and not necessarily to every individual investigator. Skills required to conduct an investigation include the ability to:

a) Obtain information from people;
b) Analyze and understand documentary evidence;
c) Understand witness confidentiality and "whistleblower" concepts;
d) Analyze and evaluate facts; make sound and objective assessments and observations; and, where appropriate, make constructive recommendations;
e) Use computer equipment, software, and related systems effectively in support of the investigative process;
f) Deliver clear, concise, accurate, and factual summaries of results of investigations, both orally and in writing;
g) Prepare and obtain signed, sworn statements; and
h) Use appropriate and authorized specialized investigative techniques.

Criminal Investigator Entry-Level Training— All OIG investigators who exercise law enforcement powers (authorized by the Inspector General Act (IG Act), section 6(c), and implemented by the Attorney General Guidelines for Offices of Inspector General, US Marshals Service deputation, or other with statutory authority) must successfully complete a formal basic training course, such as the Criminal Investigator Training Program at the Federal Law Enforcement Training Center. As an alternative, this training requirement may be satisfied by completion of a comparable course of instruction.

In addition, OIG investigators exercising law enforcement powers should attend a formal OIG-specific follow-on training program, such as the Inspector General Investigator Training Program at the Inspector General Investigator Academy (IGCIA), or equivalent, or in case of experienced criminal investigators hired from Federal law enforcement agencies outside the IG community, the IG Transitional Training Program at the IGCIA or equivalent.

Each agency should also provide orientation training (formal or informal) specifically relating to the agency's mission, programs, policies, procedure, rules, and regulations. Agencies may also consider in-service training covering similar topics, as best suits the agency's requirements and the investigator's experience. (See Appendix A, "Job Task Illustration for Investigators.")

Firearms Qualification—OIGs must ensure that all criminal investigators authorized to carry a firearm train and qualify regularly, as defined by the Attorney General Guidelines or other authoritative guidelines.

The agency must develop a policy that ensures compliance with regular firearms qualification. Such policy should address occasions when failure to qualify or attend periodic training is justified and the corrective actions taken when failure was not justified. OIG policies should require the surrender of a firearm or suspension of law enforcement authority if the failure reaches an unacceptable level.

OIGs must implement an inventory control system for firearms and related equipment, law enforcement credentials/identification, and specialized technical equipment.

Periodic Training Requirements—OIGs should also periodically train criminal investigators on effective and appropriate use of force and constitutional law and other topics articulated in the Attorney General Guidelines or other authoritative guidelines. Additional topics to consider are new laws and court decisions affecting operations; technological improvements; and any changes in agency and national level policies, procedures, rules, and regulations (e.g., Transportation Security Administration (TSA) training on "flying while armed").

All post-basic training should be part of a systematic, progressive, and documented plan to maintain the requisite knowledge, skills, and abilities. OIGs deliver such training depending on the organization's needs and mission requirements. The frequency and nature of such training may be adjusted depending on whether the investigator is in a primary or secondary position.

OIG policies should determine the frequency of, and ensure compliance with, its recurring and periodic training, which, absent unique circumstances, should not exceed 3 years.

Professional Development—The training of an investigator should be a continuing process. An investigator should receive formal and on-the-job exposure prior to an assignment requiring independent application of a given subject matter. A continuous career development program should be established to provide the proper preparation, training, and guidance to develop into professionally qualified investigators and supervisors.

To facilitate this effort, the investigative agency should develop a training profile that will satisfy its needs and consider a mentoring program. (See Appendix B, "Training Profile Illustration.")

B. INDEPENDENCE

The second general standard for investigative organizations is:

> *In all matters relating to investigative work, the investigative organization must be free, both in fact and appearance, from impairments to independence; must be organizationally independent; and must maintain an independent attitude.*

This standard places upon agencies, investigative organizations, and investigators the responsibility for maintaining independence, so that decisions used in obtaining evidence, conducting interviews, and making recommendations will be impartial and will be viewed as impartial by knowledgeable third parties. There are three general classes of impairments to independence: personal, external, and organizational.

Guidelines

Personal Impairments—Circumstances may occur in which an investigator may experience difficulty in achieving impartiality because of their views and/or personal situations and relationships. These impairments may include the following:

1. Official, professional, personal, or financial relationships that might affect the extent of the inquiry; limit disclosure of information; or weaken the investigative work in any way;
2. Preconceived opinions of individuals, groups, organizations or objectives of a particular program that could bias the investigation;
3. Previous involvement in a decisionmaking or management capacity that would affect current operations of the entity or program being investigated;
4. Biases, including those induced by political or social convictions that result from employment in, or loyalty to, a particular group or organization; and
5. Financial interest in an individual, an entity, or a program being investigated.

External Impairments— Factors external to the investigative organization may restrict its ability to conduct an independent and objective investigation and issue reports of investigation. Such factors include:

1. Interference in the assignment of cases or investigative personnel;
2. Restriction on funds or other resources dedicated to the investigation or to investigative organizations;
3. Influence on the extent and thoroughness of the investigative scope, the way in which the investigation is conducted, the individual(s) who should be interviewed, the evidence that should be obtained, and the content of the investigative report; and
4. Denial of access to sources of information, including documents and records.

Organizational Impairments—An investigative organization's independence can be affected by its position within the hierarchical structure of the subject Government entity. To help achieve maximum independence, the investigative function should be positioned outside the staff or reporting line of the unit or employees under investigation. Investigations of OIG personnel should always reflect a special sensitivity to this issue of independence.

C. DUE PROFESSIONAL CARE

The third general standard for investigative organizations is:

> *Due professional care must be used in conducting investigations and in preparing related reports.*

This standard requires a constant effort to achieve quality and professional performance. It does not imply infallibility or absolute assurances that an investigation will reveal the truth of a matter.

Guidelines

This standard requires:

Thoroughness—All investigations must be conducted in a diligent and complete manner, and reasonable steps should be taken to ensure that pertinent issues are sufficiently resolved and to ensure that all appropriate criminal, civil, contractual, or administrative remedies are considered.

Legal Requirements—Investigations should be initiated, conducted, and reported in accordance with (a) all applicable laws, rules, and regulations; (b) guidelines from the Department of Justice and other prosecuting authorities; and (c) internal agency policies and procedures. Investigations should be conducted with due respect for the rights and privacy of those involved.

Appropriate Techniques—Specific methods and techniques used in each investigation should be appropriate for the circumstances and objectives.

Impartiality—All investigations must be conducted in a fair and equitable manner, with the perseverance necessary to determine the facts.

Objectivity—Evidence must be gathered and reported in an unbiased and independent manner in an effort to determine the validity of an allegation or to resolve an issue. This includes inculpatory and exculpatory information.

Ethics—At all times, the actions of the investigator and the investigative organization must conform with all applicable standards of ethical conduct.

Timeliness—All investigations should be conducted and reported in a timely manner. This is especially critical given the impact investigations have on the lives of individuals and activities of organizations. Hence, the effectiveness of an investigator depends, in part, on the promptness of finished work products, such as prepared findings and memorialized witness interviews.

Accurate and Complete Documentation—The investigative report findings and accomplishments (indictments, convictions, recoveries, etc.) must be supported by adequate documentation (investigator notes, court orders of judgment and commitment, suspension or debarment notices, settlement agreements, etc.) and maintained in the case file.

Documentation of Policies and Procedures—To facilitate due professional care, organizations should establish written investigative policies and procedures via handbook, manual, directives, or similar mechanisms that are revised regularly according to evolving laws, regulations, and executive orders.

QUALITY STANDARDS FOR INVESTIGATIONS

QUALITATIVE STANDARDS

Qualitative standards address four critical standards that must be addressed if the effort is to be successful. These are: planning, execution, reporting, and information management.

A. PLANNING

The first qualitative standard for investigative organizations is:

> *Organizational and case-specific priorities must be established and objectives developed to ensure that individual case tasks are performed efficiently and effectively.*

Priorities and objectives apply to investigative organizations, in general (the types and numbers of investigations conducted, application of resources, minimal case-opening thresholds, etc.) and to specific investigative tasks in particular (the person(s) to interview, the records to review, and time frames for completing tasks, etc.). This standard may best be achieved by preparing organizational and case-specific plans and strategies.

Guidelines

Organizational Planning—When feasible, OIG should prepare goal-oriented annual investigative plans that are consistent with prevailing law, Attorney General Guidelines (if applicable), and OIG-specific mission and goals. Planning documents should present each organization's goals and objectives, performance measures, and a guide for managers to implement these plans. The plans should project the allocation of resources, identify priorities, describe investigative programs, and include any new initiatives. Such plans may be part of an annual appropriation request or part of the overall OIG annual plan or performance document.

Annual plans should be flexible enough to accommodate individual agency needs and the shifting of investigative priorities and staff resources, as circumstances dictate. However, operational plans should be specific enough to provide a basis for the professional management of investigative resources and workloads during the planning year.

Individual Case Planning—Upon receipt, each complaint must be evaluated against the investigative functions, priorities, and guidelines for one of three decisions:

- Initiate investigative activity,
- Refer to another appropriate authority, or
- Take no further specific investigative action.

If the decision is to initiate an investigation, the organization should begin any necessary immediate actions and establish, if appropriate, an investigative plan of action (whether verbal or written) as soon as possible. The plan should describe as many of the following components as deemed necessary:

1. Primary nature and complexity of the allegations (criminal, civil, and/or administrative);
2. Planned focus and objectives of the investigation;
3. Possible violation(s) of law, rule, or regulation and the corresponding elements of proof or standards;
4. Coordination with appropriate authorities, if warranted (another OIG, the Federal Bureau of Investigation, etc.);
5. Applicable judicial venue and coordination with prosecutors, when appropriate;
6. Steps necessary to meet investigative objectives; and
7. Resources necessary to meet investigative requirements.

During the investigation, organizations should, when appropriate, also consider the actions suggested below to ensure that the investigation is conducted efficiently and effectively (the list is not exhaustive, but representative).

1. Use of a time-phased approach that ensures that individual leads are pursued on a timely basis and that periodic evaluations of progress occur. This would include an ongoing affirmative decision to continue or terminate the investigation.
2. Identification of any causative factors that should be reported as weaknesses or internal control issues requiring corrective action by agency management.
3. Ongoing coordination with appropriate agency or other Government officials if notable security or public health and safety issues are raised.

B. EXECUTING INVESTIGATIONS

The second qualitative standard for investigative organizations is:

> *Investigations must be conducted in a timely, efficient, thorough, and objective manner.*

The investigator is a fact-gatherer and should not allow conjecture, unsubstantiated opinion, bias, or personal observations or conclusions to affect work assignments. He or she also has a duty to be receptive to evidence that is exculpatory, as well as incriminating. The investigator should collect and analyze evidence through a number of techniques, including, but not limited to, interviews of complainants, witnesses, victims, and subjects; reviews of records; surveillance and consensual monitoring; undercover operations; and use of computer technology.

Guidelines

The following guidelines should be considered, recognizing that investigations are often fluid and unpredictable:

Conducting Interviews—A review of known information should precede a planned interview. An investigator should identify himself/herself to the interviewee and state the purpose of the interview, if appropriate. Appropriate warnings[3] should be provided to those individuals suspected of violating law or regulation. Witnesses generally do not require rights advisement. When conducting an interview, particular attention should be given to obtaining the interviewee's observations and knowledge of incidents and actions or statements of other persons connected with the event. Interviewees should be asked to provide, or identify the location of, relevant documents. All interviews are subject to inclusion in reports. Any contemporaneous interview notes that are prepared in a criminal investigation should be retained as required by law or agency policy. Requests for witness confidentiality should be honored, in accordance with the IG Act and to the extent legally permissible. In all cases, interviews should be properly documented.

Collecting Evidence—Evidence should be collected in such a way as to ensure that all known or obviously relevant material is obtained, the chain of custody is preserved, and the evidence is admissible in any subsequent proceeding. The validity of information and evidence obtained during an investigation should be verified. A procedure for the disposal of physical evidence by an independent party must be followed. When using the work of a specialist, such as criminal laboratory examiners, computer forensic examiners, and financial experts, investigators should assess the specialist's ability to perform and report on the work in an impartial manner and should understand the scope and objective required of the specialist. Investigators should also consider the specialist's professional certification, experience, and relevant standards.

Documenting Activities—The results of investigative activities should be accurately and completely documented in the case file. Internal investigative guidelines should specifically and clearly address due diligence and timeliness of the documentation.

---

[3] For further details, see *Miranda* v. *Arizona*, 384 U.S. 436 (1966); *Kalkine* v. *United States*, 473 F.2d 1391, 1393, (Cr. Cl. 1973); *Garrity* v. *New Jersey*, 385 U.S. 493, 500 (1967). Also consult agency requirements related to other rights, such as *NASA* v. *FLRA* (98-369) 527 U.S. 229 (1999) 120 F.3d 1208 (Weingarten).

Complying With Legal Requirements—Interviews, evidence collection, and other activities must be initiated, conducted, and reported in accordance with all applicable laws, rules, regulations and should be conducted with due respect for the rights and privacy of those involved. This includes, for example, appropriate warnings and assurances and Grand Jury restrictions.

Additional considerations during an investigation may include:

- Obtaining, securing, and properly using Grand Jury information;
- Using parallel civil and criminal proceedings;
- Respecting the Right to Financial Privacy Act;
- Developing and using confidential informants and other sources of information;
- Obtaining and using hotline information;
- Using IG subpoenas;
- Serving as liaison and interacting with prosecutors; and
- Storing and handling electronic data.

Conducting Progress Reviews—Supervisory reviews of case activities should occur periodically to ensure that the case is progressing in an efficient, effective, thorough, and objective manner.

C. REPORTING

The third qualitative standard for investigative organizations is:

> *Reports (oral and written) must thoroughly address all relevant aspects of the investigation and be accurate, clear, complete, concise, logically organized, timely, and objective.*

All reports should accurately, clearly, and concisely reflect the relevant results of the investigator's efforts. Facts should be presented in straightforward, grammatically correct language and should avoid the use of unnecessary, obscure, and confusing verbiage. Graphics should be well-prepared, clearly relevant to the investigation, and supportive of the presentation.

Guidelines

Organizations should determine the most appropriate report mechanism (verbal or written) and format, on the basis of the circumstances of the issue(s) involved. In pursuing this standard, the following guidelines should be considered:

1. In any report, the facts should be set forth to facilitate reader comprehension.

This should include a clear and concise statement of the facts and applicable law, rule, or regulation that was allegedly violated or that formed the basis for an investigation.

2. The principles of good report writing should be followed. A quality report will be logically organized, accurate, complete, concise, impartial, and clear and should be issued in a timely manner.

3. Reports should contain exculpatory evidence and relevant mitigating information when discovered during any administrative investigation. Exculpatory evidence in a criminal or civil investigation must be brought to the attention of the assigned prosecutor.

4. Evidence outlined in a report should be supported by documentation in the investigative case file.

5. In some cases, it may be appropriate to note specific allegations that were not investigated to ensure that decisionmakers can take further action as they deem appropriate.

6. The outcome or accomplishment (fines, savings, recoveries, indictments, convictions, suspensions and debarments, or management recommendations, etc.) should be documented in the file.

7. Systemic weaknesses or management problems disclosed in an investigation should be reported to agency officials as soon as practicable.

D. MANAGING INVESTIGATIVE INFORMATION

The fourth qualitative standard for investigations is:

> *Investigative data must be stored in a manner that allows effective retrieval, reference, and analysis, while ensuring the protection of sensitive data (i.e., personally identifiable, confidential, proprietary, or privileged information or materials.).*

One of the many hallmarks of an efficient organization is its ability to retrieve information that it has collected. An effective information management system creates and enhances institutional memory. This, in turn, enhances the entire organization's ability to conduct pattern and trend analyses and to fulfill the mandate of detection and prevention. Such a system also assists in making informed judgments relative to resource allocation, training needs, investigative program development, prevention activities, and implementation of the investigative process. Further, the IG Act requires that certain data elements be reported in the semiannual reports to Congress.[4]

---

[4] OIGs are encouraged to consult the IG Act for those requirements.

Guidelines

The degree to which an organization efficiently achieves its goals is affected by the quality and relevance of information that is collected, stored, retrieved, and analyzed. Information, or the lack of it, has direct influence on management's ability to make sound decisions relating to investigative matters. Therefore, written directives should exist that define the organizational component responsible for record maintenance and the specific procedures to be performed.

Information Flow—Accurate processing of information is essential to the mission of an investigative organization. It should begin with the orderly, systematic, accurate, and secure maintenance of a management information system. Written guidance should define the data elements to be recorded in the system. The guidance should be based on legal requirements and needs and should cover the proper security and storage of personally identifiable and other sensitive information and the storage of discoverable information.

Complaint-Handling Activities—The investigative process often begins with a complaint from an individual. The initial complaint will rarely provide the agency with all the necessary information and may be the first indication of a serious violation of law. Policies, procedures, and instructions for handling and processing complaints should be in place. Individuals receiving complaints should obtain all pertinent details. The agency should adopt procedures to ensure that basic information is recorded, held confidential, and tracked to final resolution.

Case Initiation—An organization should establish guidelines, including the level of the approving authority, for making a determination to initiate an investigation or to pursue another course of action. Case assignments should be based on resource considerations, geographical dispersion and level of experience of personnel, and current workloads. A decision not to investigate (refer to another entity or take no action) should be documented.

Management Information System —Management should have certain information available to perform its responsibilities, measure its accomplishments, and respond to requests by appropriate external customers. Items that may be considered for tracking purposes include, but are not limited to, the following:

Workload Data

- Number of complaints handled;
- Cases opened;
- Cases closed;
- Cases pending (active);

- Referrals to program managers and outcomes of such referrals;
- Referrals to other investigative agencies (Federal, State, or local, including agency name);
- Referrals (criminal, civil, and administrative)
    - -accepted and
    - -declined; and
- Amount of direct and indirect labor-hours expended on each case, where appropriate.

Identification Data

- Appropriate dates (allegation received, case opened, case closed, etc.);
- Source information (anonymous, private citizen, etc.);
- Type of violations investigated (criminal, civil, administrative, etc.);
- Category of investigation (contract and grant fraud, theft, bribery, environmental violation, cybercrime, scientific misconduct, etc.);
- Priority (routine, high priority, special interest, etc.);
- Potential violations (Title 18 of the U.S. Code, agency regulations, etc.);
- Suspected dollar loss, where appropriate;
- Joint and task force investigations;
- Operation, program, office, or facility impacted (Departmental bureau or organization);
- Principal State and location where investigation is centered, including judicial venue;
- Investigative techniques employed (consensual monitoring, undercover investigation, searches, hazardous interviews and activities, etc.); and
- Indices of subjects, witnesses, and other individuals.

Investigative Results Data

- Number of indictments, convictions, declinations/acceptances, criminal outcomes, and civil actions;
- Amount of recoveries, restitutions, fines, and settlements;
- Reports issued (to prosecutors and agency management);
- Recommendations to agency management for corrective action(s) (take disciplinary action, recover monies, correct internal control weaknesses, etc.);
- Number of disciplinary or other administrative agency actions (terminations, suspensions, debarments, and personnel and contractor actions); and
- Calculated savings from the investigation, if applicable.

The above data will generally allow for the design of a basic system of administrative checks and controls to meet management needs. Depending on the complexity and scope of an investigative activity, additional data can be developed that will enable trend and pattern analyses.

16

Investigative File—All investigative activity, both exculpatory and incriminating, should be recorded in an official case file. A case file may be paper, electronic, or both and should be established upon the opening and assignment of an investigation. The file is used to maintain investigative records (interview writeups, data analysis, reports, etc.). Written directives for file management should specify procedures for at least the following:

- File organization, maintenance, storage, and security;
- Assignment of case numbers;
- Preparation and filing of documents and exhibits;
- Collection and storage of evidence;
- Distribution and dissemination of reports;
- Access control of the files;
- Retention of records, including evidence, interview writeups, investigator notes, and other case file documentation (to be determined on the basis of agency requirements, Federal records regulations, and judicial decisions);
- Ensuring that sensitive information is protected (personally identifiable information, Privacy Act information, Grand Jury information, national security information, etc.); and
- Adequate physical and logical controls over electronic case files, to include backup procedures and protection from cyberthreats.

APPENDICES

Appendix A

JOB TASK ILLUSTRATION FOR INVESTIGATORS

Receipt, Analysis, and Disposition of Allegations(s)

- Obtain data from complainant or source
- Document complaint in writing
- Know prosecutive or regulatory criteria
- Identify violations (elements of crime) or administrative standards
- Review and identify significant information or potential evidence
- Determine correct disposition of complaint (criminal, civil, or administrative)
- Open investigation, if appropriate, and coordinate with appropriate authorities (internally/externally)

Assessment, Focus, and Preparation of Investigative Plan

- Review available information and evidence
- Review legal decisions and guidelines
- Review agency programs, operational policies, and procedures
- Determine focus and scope of investigation
- Assess and identify required resources
- Identify potential witnesses, suspects, relevant documents, and evidence
- Organize and prioritize investigative activities
- Prepare initial investigative plan

Conduct Investigation

- Maintain focus and follow investigative plan (revise as necessary)
- Prepare for anticipated investigative activities (interviews, taking statements)
- Apply knowledge of laws and/or regulations
- Understand and apply techniques to ensure constitutional rights
- Project a professional image
- Use good oral and written communicative skills
- Know evidentiary rules
- Collect, analyze, and preserve evidence
- Use appropriate specialized techniques (search warrants, forensics, consensual monitoring)
- Conduct reviews and data inquiries and promptly document such activities
- Collect and analyze financial data
- Assess progress and re-focus when necessary
- Coordinate progress with supervisor (prosecutors or management, as appropriate)

- Maintain appropriate liaison
- Effectively manage the case and assist personnel and meet planned milestones
- Obtain IG or grand jury subpoenas and/or testify before grand jury

Review, Organize, and Evaluate Investigative Findings

- Review and understand the information gathered
- Organize the information and evidence gathered
- Correlate data, witnesses, and records
- Consider internal/external customer needs

Draft Report, Validate Contents, and Submit Final Report

- Write draft report--ensure accuracy, thoroughness, objectivity, proper format, clarity, and correct grammar
- Review report to ensure information is correct and complete
- Consider issues such as confidentiality, the Privacy Act, the Freedom of Information Act, and security classification
- Include disclosure caveats where appropriate
- Write final report
- Distribute to appropriate entities

Post-Investigative Tasks

- Know rules of criminal and/or civil procedure
- Assist with preparation for court/administrative proceedings
- Serve witness subpoenas
- Assist U.S. Attorney/District Attorney at trial
- Testify at trial
- Document and report results, dispositions, and outcomes
- Obtain disposition of exhibits and evidence after trial/hearing
- Return and document proper disposition of documents and evidence
- Review the organization of investigative files for efficient retrieval
- Archive investigative files
- Ensure information management database reflects accurate and final case information

Appendix B

TRAINING PROFILE ILLUSTRATION FOR INVESTIGATORS

Basic/Entry Level Training – GS 5/7[1]	CITP[2]	IGITP[3]
Administering Rights Warnings	X	
Agent Liability	X	
Basic Computer Applications	X	
Cardiopulmonary Resuscitation	X	
Complaint Assessment	X	
Ethics and Code of Conduct	X	
Federal Rules of Criminal/Civil Procedure	X	
Informants	X	
Sexual Harassment/Diversity	X	
Surveillance	X	
Testifying in Court and Trial Processes	X	
Victim/Witness Awareness	X	
Affidavits and Statements	X	X
Applying and Executing of Search Warrants	X	X
Arrest Techniques	X	X
Assisting US Attorneys and other Prosecutors	X	X
Authority and Jurisdiction	X	X
Case Development and Liaison	X	X
Collection, Protection, and Rules of Evidence	X	X
Communication Skills (Oral and Written)	X	X
Constitutional Rights	X	X
Defensive Tactics	X	X
Disclosure/Privacy/FOIA	X	X
Electronic Sources of Information	X	X
Elements of a Crime	X	X
Firearms Proficiency	X	X
Fraud Schemes	X	X
Interviewing Techniques	X	X
Investigative Planning	X	X
Relevant Civil and Criminal Statutes	X	X
Report Writing	X	X
Use of Electronic Evidence	X	X
Administrative Remedies		X
Civil Remedies		X
Concepts of Confidentiality		X
Employee Complainants		X
Inspector General Act		X
Inspector General Subpoena		X
Whistleblower Protections		X

---

[1] On-the Job or In-Service Training should, to some degree, be provided for each of these areas based on the organization's mission and needs.

[2] Criminal Investigator Training Program conducted by the Federal Law Enforcement Training Center.

[3] Inspector General Basic Training Program conducted by the Inspector General Criminal Investigator Academy.

Agency In-Service Training

Recurring[4]
    Code of Conduct
    Sexual Harassment/Diversity
    Ethics
    Agency Authority/Jurisdiction
    Physical Efficiency Battery
    Health Assessment
Quarterly
    Firearms Familiarization and Qualification
    Use of Force Policy (including Deadly Force)
Periodic[5]
    Legal Update (Criminal and Civil)
    Arrest Techniques
    Defensive Tactics
    Intermediate Weapons
    Cardiopulmonary Resuscitation
    Lifestyle Management/Stress
    Victim/Witness Awareness
    Blood Borne Pathogens (annually)

---

[4] Based on agency requirements.
[5] Conducted on a scheduled basis in accordance with applicable standards (e.g., Attorney General guidelines, Federal regulations, etc.).

Advanced Training[6]	GS-7	GS-9	GS-11	GS-12	GS-13	GS-14
Data Analysis	X	X				
Employee Conduct and Integrity	X	X				
Financial Fraud (Loans, Credit Cards, etc.)		X				
Accounting Principles		X				
Embezzlement		X				
Environmental Crimes		X				
Computer Crimes		X				
Bribery		X				
Contract and Grant Fraud		X				
Technical Investigative Equipment		X				
Advanced Interviewing		X				
Undercover Operations		X				
Advanced Financial Investigations			X			
Advanced Computer Applications			X			
Electronic Evidence Extraction			X			
Electronic Evidence Analysis			X			
Anti-Trust Investigations			X			
1st-Level Supervision				X	X	
Case Management				X	X	
Problem Solving and Conflict Resolution					X	
Advanced Supervision					X	
Leadership, Coaching, and Mentoring					X	
Office Administration/ Management					X	
Personnel Management						X

---

[6] Based on organization's needs and mission requirements.

Appendix C
Non-Exhaustive Table of Legislation, Executive Orders, Standards, Regulations, and Other Guidance for Investigators

Document	Description
1. Legislation	
Crimes, 18 U.S.C. §§ 1-2725 and Criminal Procedure, 18 U.S.C. §§ 3001-3771	Establishes crimes and criminal procedures as they pertain to OIG oversight of departmental programs.
Electronic Communications Protection Act, 18 U.S.C. §§ 2510-2522 (Wiretap Statute)	Limits the ability of law enforcement officers to intercept electronic communications without judicial authorization, and regulates the use and disclosure of information obtained through authorized wiretaps.
False Claims Act, 31 U.S.C. §§ 3729-3733 et seq. (P.L. 99-562)	Establishes civil liability for fraudulent claims submitted to the Federal Government.
Family Educational Rights and Privacy Act (FERPA), 20 U.S.C. § 1232g	Imposes additional restrictions on the use of administrative subpoenas to obtain educational records from an educational agency or institution.
Federal Conflict of Interest Laws, 18 U.S.C. §§ 202-209	Establishes criminal conflict of interest penalties for Federal employees.
Federal Tort Claims Act, 28 U.S.C. §§ 1346(b), 2671-80	Authorizes the public to bring civil lawsuits against the Federal Government for the negligent acts of Federal employees within the scope of their employment that cause injury to person or property.
Freedom of Information Act, as amended, 5 U.S.C. § 552 (P.L. 104-231)	Allows members of the public to obtain Federal records subject to certain exemptions (including exemptions for certain investigative information).
Health Insurance Portability and Accountability Act of 1996, 29 U.S.C. § 1181 (P.L. 104-191)	Protects the privacy of confidential personally identifiable medical information.
The Inspector General Act of 1978, as amended, 5 U.S.C. App. 3 (P.L. 95-452); Inspector General Reform Act of 2008, (P.L. 110-409)	Establishes independent and objective Offices of Inspector General; establishes IG subpoena power and other authorities.
Law Enforcement Availability Pay Act of 1994, 5 U.S.C. § 5545a	Authorizes additional pay to criminal investigators to ensure availability for unscheduled official duties.
Law Enforcement Officers Safety Act of 2003, Chapter 44, 18 U.S.C. § 926 B-C (P.L. 108-277)	Authorizes qualified law enforcement officers (including certain qualified retired officers) to carry a concealed firearm.
Pen/Trap Statute, 18 U.S.C. § 3121	Requires government entities to obtain a warrant before collecting real-time information, such as dialing, routing, and addressing information related to communications.
Privacy Act, 5 U.S.C. § 552a (P.L. 93-579)	Protects personal individual information held by Federal agencies, and authorizes individuals to obtain and to seek corrections to those records.

Procurement Integrity Act, 41 U.S.C. § 423	Prohibits the release of source selection and contractor bid or personal information and sets conflict of interest requirements for procurement personnel.
Program Fraud Civil Remedies Act, 31 U.S.C. § 3801 et seq.	Establishes an administrative process to allow Federal agencies to recover for fraudulent claims to the agency of up to $150,000.
Right to Financial Privacy Act, 12 U.S.C. § 3401 et seq.	Requires that agencies provide individuals and partnerships with five or fewer partners with notice and an opportunity to object before a financial institution can disclose personal financial information in response to an administrative subpoena.
Stored Communications Act, 18 U.S.C. §§ 2701-2712	Limits the Government's ability to obtain stored account information from network service providers such as ISPs.
Trade Secrets Act, 18 U.S.C. § 1905	Prohibits government employees from disclosing certain confidential or proprietary business information.
Victim and Witness Protection Act of 1982, 18 U.S.C. §§ 1512-1515	Defines tampering with a witness, victim, or informant; requires Federal law enforcement agencies to have guidelines and policies to provide services to victims of crimes.
Whistleblower Protection Act, 5 U.S.C. § 1204, 22 U.S.C. § 4137	Protects the rights of, and prevents retaliation against, Federal employees who disclose governmental fraud, waste, abuse, and other improper activity.
5 U.S.C. §§ 8425(b), 8335	Authorizes agencies to exempt law enforcement officers from mandatory retirement at age 57 with 20 years of covered law enforcement service.
41 U.S.C. § 265	Prevents retaliation against contractor employees for certain disclosures of information relating to a substantial violation of law related to a contract.
2. Executive Orders	
Administrative Allegations Against Inspectors General, Exec. Order No. 12993, 61 Fed. Reg. 13043 (March 21,1996)	Directs the PCIE and ECIE Integrity Committee to receive, review, and refer for investigation allegations of wrongdoing against IGs and certain staff members of OIGs (Note – superseded by passage of the Inspector General Reform Act of 2008).
Integrity and Efficiency in Federal Programs, Exec. Order No. 12805, 57 Fed. Reg. 20627 (May 11, 1992)	Establishes the PCIE and ECIE and describes their functions and responsibilities (note—superseded by passage of the Inspector General Reform Act of 2008).
Principles of Ethical Conduct for Government Officers and Employees, Exec. Order 12731, 55 Fed. Reg. 42547 (October 17, 1990)	Lays out principles of ethical conduct, Office of Government Ethics authority, agency responsibilities, delegations of authority, and general provisions.

3. Standards	
PCIE/ECIE Quality Standards for Federal Offices of Inspector General (Oct. 2003)	Establishes standards for the management, operation, and conduct of the Federal Offices of Inspector General.
Standards of Ethical Conduct for Employees of the Executive Branch, 5 CFR Part 2635 (June 2009)	Establishes general principles for ethical conduct of employees of the Executive Branch.
4. Other Guidance and Regulations	
Attorney General Guidelines for Domestic FBI Operations (Sept. 29, 2008)	Addresses the broad operational areas of the FBI's methods of investigative and intelligence gathering, including coordination, analysis and planning.
Attorney General Guidelines for Offices of Inspector General with Statutory Law Enforcement Authority (Dec. 8, 2003)	Governs the law enforcement authorities of OIGs that have been granted statutory law enforcement power from the Attorney General.
Attorney General's Guidelines on FBI Undercover Operations (Nov. 13, 1992)	Covers authorization of undercover operations, protecting innocent parties against entrapment, and monitoring and control of undercover operations.
Attorney General Guidelines Regarding the Use of Confidential Informants (May 2002)	Applies to the use of confidential informants in criminal investigations and prosecutions by Department of Justice law enforcement agencies and Federal prosecuting officers.
Attorney General Memorandum for the Heads and Inspectors General of Executive Departments and Agencies re: Procedures for Lawful, Warrantless Monitoring of Verbal Communications (May 30, 2002)	Revises and updates rules and procedures for obtaining authorization to intercept verbal communications without the consent of all parties to the communication, as well as the procedures for consensual monitoring where no written authorization is required.
Attorney General Order No. 3168-2010 – Authorization for the Federal Offices of Inspector General to Provide Mutual Assistance in the Execution of Search and Arrest Warrants (June 28, 2010)	Authorizes and sets conditions on OIG sharing of agents to seek and execute search, seizure or arrest warrants.
Attorney General Policy Regarding the Disclosure to Prosecutors of Potential Impeachment Information Concerning Law Enforcement Agency Witnesses ("*Giglio* Policy") (Dec. 9, 1996)	Ensures that prosecutors receive sufficient information to meet their disclosure obligations under *Giglio v. United States*, while protecting the legitimate privacy rights of Government employees.
CIGIE Guidelines on Undercover Operations (June 2010)	Provides guidance on certain undercover operations in accordance with the Attorney General's Guidelines for Offices of Inspectors General.

CIGIE Qualitative Assessment Review Guidelines Federal Offices of Inspector General (Investigation Divisions) (May 2009)	Provides guidance on conducting external qualitative assessment reviews of OIG investigative operations.
CIGIE Procedures to Obtain Assistance From Another OIG In the Execution of Search and Arrest Warrants (Nov. 15, 2010)	Establishes procedures for OIG sharing of agents for search, seizure or arrest warrants.
Deputy Attorney General Guidance for Prosecutors Regarding Criminal Discovery (Jan. 10, 2010)	Provides guidance for prosecution team members (including IG agents) on the government's legal discovery obligations, including discovery of exculpatory and impeachment information as applied to electronic communications.
Deputy Attorney General Guidance on the Use, Prevention, and Disclosure of Electronic Communications in Federal Criminal Cases (March 30, 2011)	Provides guidance for prosecution team members (including IG agents) on legal discovery obligations relating to electronic communications among members of the prosecution team, victims and witnesses.
Deputy Attorney General Memorandum to Inspectors General Directing Them to Refer Potential Violations of Federal Privacy Statutes to the Department of Justice for Investigation and Prosecution (Oct. 18, 1999)	Directs Inspectors General to refer 18 U.S.C. § 1030(a)(2) offenses to the Computer Crimes and Intellectual Property Section in the Criminal Division; Tax Offenses to the Criminal Enforcement Office in the Tax Division; and Privacy Act Violations to the Public Integrity Section in the Criminal Division.
Federal Rules of Criminal Procedure, R. 1-17	Federal court rules governing preliminary proceedings, the grand jury, indictment, arraignment, and preparation for trial.
Federal Rules of Evidence, §§ 101-1103	Federal court rules for introduction of evidence in criminal or civil trials.
2 C.F.R. Part 180 OMB Guidelines to Agencies on Governmentwide Debarment and Suspension (Nonprocurement)	Establishes causes, procedure and treatment of government-wide suspension and debarment for non-procurement (e.g., loan, guarantee, insurance and grant) actions. Please note individual agency adoption pieces in 2 C.F.R Subtitle B.
5 C.F.R. Part 731.204-05	Establishes causes and procedure for debarment from federal employment.
48 C.F.R. Subpart 3.9	Provides whistleblower protections for contractor employees and sets procedures for filing complaints, investigating complaints, and remedies.
48 C.F.R. Part 9.4 Procurement Suspension and Debarment Regulations	Establishes causes, procedure and treatment of government-wide suspension and debarment for procurement actions.
49 CFR § 1544.219: TSA Regulation regarding carriage of accessible weapons	Sets out situations when it is permissible for a law enforcement officer to carry a weapon aboard a plane.

Appendix D

The QSI working group consisted of the following AIGIs:

John E. Brennan, II, TVA OIG
John E. Dupuy, DOI OIG
Karen L. Ellis, USDA OIG
Jay Hodes, HHS OIG
Aaron R. Jordan, PBGC OIG
Joseph A. McMillan, NRC OIG

Investigations Committee Members

Chair:	Carl W. Hoecker	IG, U.S. Capitol Police
Co-chair:	Eric M. Thorson	IG, Treasury Department
Members:	Lanie D'Alessandro	IG, National Reconnaissance Office
	Charles K. Edwards	Acting IG, Department of Homeland Security
	Arthur A. Elkins	IG, Environmental Protection Agency
	Donald A. Gambatesa	IG, Agency for International Development
	J. Russell George	IG, Treasury Inspector General for Tax Administration
	Peggy E. Gustafson	IG, Small Business Administration
	Allison C. Lerner	IG, National Science Foundation
	John P. McCarty	Acting IG, Department of Housing and Urban Development
	Brian D. Miller	IG, General Services Administration
	George J. Opfer	IG, Veterans Administration
	Jon T. Rymer	IG, Federal Deposit Insurance Corporation
	Cynthia A. Schnedar	Acting IG, Department of Justice
	Karl W. Schornagel	IG, Library of Congress
	Kathleen S. Tighe	IG, Department of Education

The following individuals contributed substantially to the final product:

William D. Hamel, AIGI, ED OIG/AIGI Committee Chair
Glenn P. Harris, General Counsel, SBA OIG
John R. Hartman, DIG, DOE OIG
Angela N. Hrdlicka, Director, IGCIA